Child's Play

poems by

Dianne Alvine

Finishing Line Press
Georgetown, Kentucky

Child's Play

Copyright © 2018 by Dianne Alvine
ISBN 978-1-63534-454-7 First Edition
All rights reserved under International and Pan-American Copyright Conventions. No part of this book may be reproduced in any manner whatsoever without written permission from the publisher, except in the case of brief quotations embodied in critical articles and reviews.

ACKNOWLEDGMENTS

Thank you to the editors of the following journals, anthologies and events in which these poems first appeared:

Child's Play was selected for the Painted Poetry IV Wall Exhibit, Surf City Library event, 2017
The Clothesline was selected for the Painted Poetry III Wall Exhibit, Surf City Library event, 2016
Oranges won a Judge's Choice Award and was featured in the Ontario Poetry Society's *Food for Thought* anthology, 2014
The Clothesline was awarded Third Place in the International Dancing Poetry Contest, 2013
Someday was included in *Forward Poetry*'s One Week Poetry Challenge anthology, 2013

Publisher: Leah Maines
Editor: Christen Kincaid
Cover Art: Dianne Alvine
Author Photo: Dianne Alvine
Cover Design: Elizabeth Maines McCleavy

Printed in the USA on acid-free paper.
Order online: www.finishinglinepress.com
also available on amazon.com

Author inquiries and mail orders:
Finishing Line Press
P. O. Box 1626
Georgetown, Kentucky 40324
U. S. A.

Table of Contents

The Clothesline 1

Ghost Town 2

Genes 3

Measuring Up 4

Someday 5

Tonsillectomy 6

Monsters 7

Thresholds 8

A Lavender Dress 9

Forsythia 10

Now, The Dogwood 11

Oranges 12

Only a Moment 13

Roses 14

Starry Night 15

Child's Play 16

For my children
Stephen, Danielle, and Lucienne

And

*For my grandmother, Lena, whose
love was unconditional.*

The Clothesline

I remember the clothesline
on the second floor of the house,
where I spent the first twelve
years of my life growing up.
I remember my mother, leaning
out the window, her hair blowing,
as she pulled in the clothes when
it started to rain. She was never
quick enough, and she'd have to
put them in a big, wicker basket,
and trudge them downstairs, to
hang in the cellar. I remember seeing
a picture taken some months after
I was born. She was hanging clothes,
and smiling like a beauty queen,
dressed in a slinky, slip of a dress,
the one she vowed she'd get into,
after she had me.
Nowadays, I am surprised and wistful
to see such a 'sighting.' It is a bitter
sweet reminder of things slipping
away. Yet, gentle memories linger…
I am a child again. I can feel the summer
heat on my back, as I pedal my bike
faster and faster. The day is crystal clear,
and as blue as my father's eyes. It's a
perfect day for hanging clothes. The sweet
scent of just cut grass fills the air. I can hear
the muffled sounds of my grandmother and
my mother's voices as I get closer and closer,
just braking my bike inches away, from
the freshly hung clothes.

Ghost Town

They are all gone now.
Mother, father, grandparents.
Once, I thought I saw them
etched in one brilliant cloud,
shoulder to shoulder,
nodding their heads in approval,
and smiling benignly.
It was only my mind playing tricks.
I just wanted to see them
one more time,
To hold them,
To tell them things
I should have said, but didn't.
Now, they inhabit
the ghost town of my heart,
where they wander aimlessly,
until I find myself bumping
into them,
my throat parched,
from so many
unanswered questions.

Genes

It always began
the same way.
Every Sunday morning
the dreaded ritual
would begin.
I would be held hostage
by my father, a man whose
brilliance with numbers
was not shared
by his daughter.
My father, the tutor,
trying to teach
my right brain
the language of mathematics.
We were light years apart———
except for biology.
I tried to make a connection,
but never could get
from point A
to point B
without my universe
collapsing.
I had no passion
for polynomial equations,
or geometric patterns.
My father had no passion
for anything else.

Measuring Up

Mother, you could have put
Betty Crocker to shame,
or, at the very least,
been her best pupil.
With your perfect pie crust
every time,
rolling the dough
just so,
using the same rolling pin
as your mother,
who passed it on to you
like a trophy.
And mother,
don't think I didn't try
to measure up
to your expectations,
but the lessons proved
tasteless
to my palate.
I have found
I do not care much
for pie,
anyway.

Someday

Father, I wish you were here
so that we could start over,
better than before.
I guess some things
are not meant to be.
You would tell me
"I love you, forever and always,
that will never change."
And my heart would say
the same.
We would laugh together
about silly things,
you would teach me
about life,
guiding me with your love.
Father, can you feel my child's kiss
planted on the door of heaven
just for you, today?
I hope so.
Please keep it tucked away
in your heart,
so that you can give it
back to me,
when we meet again,
someday.

Tonsillectomy

'Today is the day
I am going to take you
to see the children,' my Mother said.
'The ones I told you about,
in the children's ward,
in the hospital.' I held her hand tightly
as she opened the heavy door,
leading me down a hallway
where a smiling lady sat behind
a large desk.
'I brought my daughter to see
the children,'
and they whispered words
I did not understand.
'Come with me,' the smiling lady said.
'The children are sleeping now,
we can not wake them,
would you like to see their room?'
I nodded, and the
smiling lady took my hand.
It was a tiny room, so bright
it hurt my eyes, there were no children,
only a man with a mask on his face
who put an orange balloon
across my nose.
When I woke, the smiling lady
and the man with the mask
were gone, there was just
my Mother,
standing over me,
smiling.

Monsters

I had a whale of a cry this morning.
It took me by surprise.
A torrential tide of tears
streamed down my face.
I couldn't stop them.
Old demons,
hidden in the crusted corners
of my life,
suddenly rose from their coffins,
where I thought I had neatly buried them,
so many years ago.
Now, they whisked me
through the labyrinth of time,
to the creaking door of my childhood.
Brazenly, they fanned the flaming embers
of a long forgotten, painful memory.
Would they never disappear?
Or would their eternal vapors
hover over me like a spirit,
not quite dead, but not yet ready,
to say goodbye.

Thresholds

I did not shed
a tear that day,
nor any day that followed.
This was the second time
we had been together
in this church.
You walked me down the aisle
the first time,
and gave me over to another
for better or for worse.
At an earlier time,
you were halfway 'round the world
fighting a war.
You did not hear my first cry.
I was not there,
when you silently
passed away.

A Lavender Dress

Lavender
was the color
of the dress,
my grandmother
was buried in.
On her feet
were the black
Reebok sneakers
she wore every day.
At her funeral,
people reminded
each other
of her strength.
I only remembered
she loved me,
when it felt like
nobody else did,
how she filled my world
with a peaceful light,
the same one
I hope she finds,
as her Reeboks carry
her safely,
into the next world.

Forsythia

'Spring has sprung,' my father used to say,
when he looked out the window,
and his eyes rested on the bright,
yellow blooms that magically
burst into life each year.
Like an asteroid shower,
thousands of majestic blossoms
filled the yard with bouquets
of golden bells.
I could hear my father sing then.
'you are my sunshine,'
his voice clear and bright,
filled with the hope
springtime can bring,
after the harshness
of winter.
My heart yearns
to hear him sing again,
to breathe life
into my spring,
as I smother myself,
in the billowy,
yellow blooms of hope.

Now, the Dogwood

is in bloom, and I see a profusion
of pink as I drive past lawns
covered by the soft, silky petals,
a feast for eyes
weary of winter grays.
It is in this season
of winter's death
that I think about you,
grandfather,
a boy who learned early
what it meant to accept
a man's responsibilities.
There were no children's games
for you, and yet,
you took such care
to make a garden of your life
that my own heart blossoms
each time I see green buds
yawn into spring,
stretching themselves
to their potential,
something you did
without ever knowing
there was such a thing.

Oranges

I screamed with silent pain
as I watched you turn into someone
I hardly knew. Each day
felt like a little death,
that trampled over my sorrowful soul.
Your eyes, that once held
A mother's love, no longer
recognized your sad-eyed child.
There was no going back now.
Whatever had been said,
or not said, was done.
Our last supper had been eaten.
Until one blessed day you cried out,
"Thirsty, please, oranges."
When you stuck out your tongue
in anticipation, I laughed so hard
I almost peed in my pants.
We became children then,
in this new game.
With each slice I'd feed you,
you'd ask for more.
I laughed, as the sticky juice
spilled from lips
that once kissed away every tear.
I laughed again
as I brushed big, fat baby kisses
all over your succulent face.
When I tucked you into bed
and kissed you goodnight,
I could smell the perfumed
scent of orange blossoms
suspended in the air,
your fragrance embracing me,
all the way home.

Only a Moment

Summer is swiftly
saying its last goodbyes.
The bees no longer
visit grandmother's azalea,
its brown blossoms forlorn
and sad, the way you felt
when she died,
tears, like an avalanche,
tumbling into eternity.
Look at the old apple tree,
its branches as withered
as grandmother's hands.
Do you remember the fragrance
of cinnamon and nutmeg swirling
in the air, the sweet taste
of apples, as intoxicating
as your first kiss.
Let this memory
roll over your tongue,
even as you kick
the rotting fruit,
the smell of decay
drowning your lungs
with sadness.
Too soon, the vast darkness
devours the light, and a chill breeze
shivers your spine.
'I love you,' you shout
into the emptiness, and wonder
if grandmother is watching,
as you run recklessly
past the monsters hiding
in the shadows,
to that little house
that has been waiting patiently,
just for your return.

Roses

Outside my window
I stare at their lovely faces.
I am a child again,
overcome with wonder,
their beauty, like red velvet
wet with dew,
bathed in morning's
first gentle light.

I want to feel
their petals
caress my face.
I want to feel
their softness
calm my beating heart.

Not so the dragonflies.
They follow me each day
as I walk home
from school.
They will knit my lips shut,
so my grandmother says.
I will tell no one
of this secret terror.
I am brave.

But, one day
I run so fast
I fall.
I can taste the blood,
as it trickles down
my face. I can see
the bright red
smears of it
on my hands.
At home, Mama asks
'what happened?'
And I tell her-
I licked all the roses,
and they tasted
beautiful.

Starry Night

As a child wishes
upon a star,
I wished to see them
one more time.
And in a dream,
on a starry night,
they rose to greet me.
And we gathered round
the same table
once again.
And with our hearts,
we joined hands.
And bowed our heads
in prayer.
And as we prayed
I heard their voices,
as clear and bright
as the stars in Van Gogh's
'Starry Night.'
And tears of thanks
tumbled down my face,
as our voices
became one,
with all the universe
and all the starry nights.

Child's Play

The leaves crunch
beneath my feet.
Above, they rain
like confetti
from a starched, blue sky.
A childhood memory swirls,
like an incandescent top,
to a day as pristine
as mother's milk.
There you are, grandmother.
Your face alive with love.
In one hand you hold
a pair of skates.
The other caresses my face.
You watch, keen as a hawk,
as I skate away from you,
down the freshly tarred street,
its once sheltering foliage
now a skeleton
of outstretched arms.
As the distance
between us lengthens,
I can feel the shadows
of the passing years
whisper their secrets.
And the rustling leaves
answer, in consolation.

Dianne has been reading, writing, and loving poetry since she was a child. She is retired now, after having worked her entire life as a social worker for people who have emotional and physical disabilities. She says they will always have a special place in her heart.

Dianne has raised three children, and has six grandchildren, who seem to be growing faster than the speed of light! In the past, Dianne has rescued several dogs and cats from a local shelter. She now lives with her rescue dog, Baby, in a quiet retirement community near the Jersey shore.

Throughout the years, Dianne has taken poetry courses and classes, both in college and on-line, and has been a participant in several different poetry groups. She's also attended poetry getaways and participated in painted poetry events in her area. Dianne is grateful for all the wonderful poets in her monthly poet's group at the Surf City Library, in Long Beach Island, N.J.

Dianne has received recognition for her poetry. Her poems have appeared in anthologies, and on-line journals. She hopes people find something to enjoy in her poems, and perhaps they can see a little bit of their own humanity in her poetry.

Dianne says she lives and breathes poetry each day of her life.

www.ingramcontent.com/pod-product-compliance
Lightning Source LLC
LaVergne TN
LVHW041526070426
835507LV00013B/1842